THE HIPPOPOTAMUS

Selected Translations 1945-1985

by

Charles Guenther

14.93

BkMk PRESS-UMKC
College of Arts & Sciences

University of Missouri-Kansas City
5216 Rockhill Rd., Rm. 204
Kansas City, MO 64110-2499

Grateful acknowledgment is made to the editors and publishers of the following magazines in which all but one of these translations (the Eskimo song, "The Hunter") first appeared in the present or earlier versions:

Accent: "Light, Light, Somewhat Revolving" (Jules Romains) **Approach:** "Time's Horses" (Jules Supervielle) **Black Mountain Review:** "The Hippopotamus" (Theophile Gautier) **Blue Unicorn:** "Fool's Song i" (Emile Verhaeren) **The Chariton Review:** "A Good-by" (Alain Bosquet) **Chelsea:** "As You Wish" (Mario Luzi) **Choice:** "The Shade of the Magnolia" and "Day and Night" (Eugenio Montale) **Climax:** "Poem" (Pablo Picasso) **Deep Channel Packet:** "The Green Comb" (Raffaele Carrieri) **Discourse:** "Tavern guitar playing a jota today" (Antonio Machado) **Driftwind:** "Larks" (Saint-Pol-Roux) **Eads Bridge:** "Cat" folio (Indiana): "The Stain" (Pierre Jean Jouve) and "At the Florist's" (Jacques Prevert) **Gallery Series Five:** "The Difficult Poem" (Jose Agustin Goytisolo) **The Galley Sail Review:** "The World Is Full of Voices" (Jules Supervielle) **Image magazine:** "With the Flashes of the Night" and "He Lit His Pipe" (Phoebus Delphis); "Insects" (Damaso Alonso) **International Anthology** (Athens): "Night" (Maria Celeste Achille Todde) **The Literary Review:** "What Do You Want?", "Stone Quarries," "In the Sense of Death," "A Buried One in Me Sings," "Woods Are Sleeping," "Cool With Sleeping Rivers," "Space," "Mirror," "In the Willow Branches," "We've Heard the Sea Again," "The Crossing," "Visible, Invisible" and "The Incomparable Earth" (Salvatore Quasimoso); " I Remember a Season" and "From The Waters of Saturday'" (Maria Luisa Spaziani); "A Woman Brought Naked," "The Art of Poetry" and "London, March 1945" (Pierre Emmanuel) **The Minnesota Review:** "Position" (Blas de Otero) **The Missouri Review:** "Sentry of the Silent" (Rene Char) **Pennsylvania Literary Review:** "On a Picture by a Chinese Painter" (Henri Michaux) **Poet Lore:** "Winter" (Antal Vizy); "On the Site of the Convent," "On the Watershed" and "Finale" (Tibor Tollas); "On An Unwritten Letter" and Seascape" (Eugenio Montale); "The Holiday Ended" (Pier Paolo Pasolini); "Pledges" (Pierre Emmanuel); "The sun is a globe of fire," "Tell me if you remember, love," "The afternoon will yet" and "Oh, figures on the portico" (Antonio Machado) **Poetry:** "The Inventors," "Put On Guard" and "Anoukis and Later Jeanne" (Rene Char) **Poetry Digest:** "Dancer" (Edgar Degas) **Quarterly Review of Literature:** "Forest," "Iguazu," "The World in Us," "Let's shield your light," "Make Room," "Memory" and "The Face" (Jules Supervielle); "On a Night Without Adornment" (Rene Char) **Sheba Review:** "My Whisper" (Eskimo song) **Stolen Paper Review:** "Fool's Song ii" (Emile Verhaeren) **Webster Review:** "A Nail for Hanging the Soul" and "He Invents a Vertigo" (Alain Bosquet); "Three Poems on Death" (Carlos Bousono) **Weid:** "Springtime" (Stephane Mallarme) **Western Humanities Review:** "The Strawberries" (Tristan Dereme)

Only two of these translations have previously appeared in book form: Antonio Machado's "Tavern guitar" in **An Anthology of Spanish Poetry**, edited by Angel Flores (Doubleday, 1961); and Mario Luzi's "As You Wish" in **Modern European Poetry**, edited by Willis Barnstone (Bantam, 1966). Like most of the magazine issues containing these translations, the latter anthologies are now out of print.

Cover illustration by Wayne Pycior.

Financial assistance for this project was provided by the Missouri Arts Council, a state agency.

Library of Congress Cataloging-in-Publication Data

The Hippopotamus: selected translations, 1945-1985.

1. Poetry, Modern—20th century—Translations into English. 2. English poetry—Translations from foreign languages. I. Guenther, Charles, 1920- . PN6101.H56 1986 808.81'04 86-3389 ISBN 0-933532-56-3

BkMk Press - UMKC

Dan Jaffe, Editor-in-Chief
Pat Huyett, Assoc. Editor
Pat Shields, Editorial Asst.

For Esther

and for my fellow craftsmen

THE HIPPOPOTAMUS shows some of the scope of Charles Guenther's translations which have appeared in hundreds of different little magazines and anthologies. But even this can't adequately show his depth and breadth. For instance, it contains nothing from his published selections from Juan Ramon Jimenez, Jules Laforgue, Paul Valery and Jean Wahl, or from his Modern Italian Poets. Nor does it contain any poems from his book manuscripts of work from Jean Cocteau, Pierre Reverdy or Leopold Sedar Senghor; or from his ms. volumes of Quebec, French Surrealist or Latin American poets, or from more recent European poets. It omits, too, almost everything before the 20th century, not only the Provençal poets he translated but also his work from Garcilaso de la Vega, Pierre de Ronsard, Leopardi and others.

—D.J.

3

Translator's Note

Literary translation is its own reward, as most translators realize or they soon quit the game. I started in my teens, to pollinate my own poetry, and vowed to stop at 25. But how can one forsake this craft on discovering its infinite nuances and needs—and knowing that so much old and new remains to be translated? For world poetry like civilization itself is marked by growth and change. The new poets arrive.

Relatively few translators were active in those early years, and colleges (many now "universities") scorned my proposals for teaching creative translation. (They still do, incidentally.) I dreamed of attacking several languages singlehandedly, and a host of editors nourished that illusion. Among those who encouraged my work in this small selection alone were Willis Barnstone, Robert Creeley, Sheila Cudahy, Wallace Fowlie, James Laughlin, Sonia Raiziss and Theodore Weiss.

Now translation has begun to flourish, and several generations of brilliant craftsmen have emerged. Most of my translations were done "raw" from texts which, as far as I knew, had never been turned into English. In 1940, for instance, I read that Supervielle was considered "the greatest living French poet," and I wrote him for permission to translate Les Amis inconnus (1934). When he told me I had done a "polishing job" on his poems I was elated. But I soon realized that one doesn't "polish" Supervielle; his strength is in his simplicity.

Whether we read or write or translate it, poetry is a game meant to be enjoyed. That's why this particular book is mostly unencumbered by scholarly notes and details. I must admit that I enjoyed Dan Jaffe's selection, for it includes some of my favorites. I hope other readers will find something here, even a poem or two, to enjoy as well.

—Charles Guenther

Contents

Spanish

INTRODUCTION

Not long ago Charles Guenther sent me a list of poets and translators he has known or befriended over the years. It included John Ciardi, Willis Barnstone, Wallace Fowlie, Laurence Lieberman, John Frederick Nims, Theodore Weiss, Richard Wilbur, Howard Nemerov, and William Jay Smith, to name a few. He said any of them might provide a brief foreword to this book. In a subsequent letter Charles requested I write the introduction, since I had "helped select the poems." I can hardly speak for all of those who have recognized the contribution to letters made by Charles Guenther. Nor can I adequately stand in for those others who might have written this short piece. As editor of BkMk Press, University of Missouri-Kansas City, I do thank Charles for allowing BkMk to publish his selected translations. Too often in our time the poet and translator feels gratitude because his work is presented. That is misplaced gratitude. Publishers and readers owe a debt to those who do the hard work of keeping literature and language alive. Charles Guenther has spent a life in the mines earning our gratitude. This book points in the direction of his devotion and achievement.

I cannot speak to the denotative accuracy of these translations. Frankly, that is not my central concern. I have read innumerable translations from different languages. Others have assured me of their accuracy and purity of intent, but, unfortunately, often I have been bored. I have had no sense of excitement, of the original poetry beyond the paraphrase. Many translations do not feel like poems in the language into which they have been transported.

Because Charles Guenther is a poet himself and because he wishes the poems he translates to move us in English no matter what language they came from I especially value his work. If a reader were to come on a well-wrought Guenther translation inadequately labeled he might not be aware it was a translation. I do not mean Charles Guenther is cavalier or insufficiently devoted to the originals, only that he remembers the poetry matters most.

This book suggests how varied are Charles Guenther's appreciations, how intense his attention, how developed his craft. But one should also remember Charles Guenther as a man. Yes, for years he has been well known as a prolific translator. He has

9

won a number of significant awards. But how many lives he has personally enriched cannot be measured. Too often Charles Guenther has been taken for granted. Whatever attention has come to him is slight compared to the attention he has lavished on other writers as a translator, reviewer, organizer, teacher, and friend. This book aims to honor Charles Guenther not only as an artist and scholar but also as an extraordinary person. Whatever praise we offer is insufficient.

Dan Jaffe
Editor-in-Chief, BkMk Press

MY WHISPER / Eskimo song

I'll sing a little song,
a song about myself.
I've been sick since last fall
and I'm weak as a boy.

    Unaya, Unaya

I want my woman
to go off to another hut
with another man
who'd take care of her,
hard and sure as winter ice.

Sadly I want her gone
with a better protector
since I haven't the strength
to get out of bed.

    Unaya, Unaya

Do you know what'll happen to you
now that I'm weak and can't get up
and only my memories are strong?

11

THE HUNTER / Eskimo song

A man went out,
he went out alone,
he walked in the cold,
in the wind,
he went to the Big Mountain.
He saw something in the snow,
not a rabbit,
not a quail,
something cold.
With hands that stuck out of the snow,
feet that stuck out of the snow,
the hands gnawed by foxes,
the feet gnawed by wolves.
The father looked at it
without a word.
He swept snow off the clothes,
he blew on the eyes,
on the mouth,
he pressed his heart,
his own against the other heart.
But his son was cold,
rock-hard,
still as ice,
and for three nights
the father went mad,
losing his path,
forgetting his way,
his light went out,
the light in his head.
Now the father sings
under the tent
with the Eskimos,
they all sing together,
they sing for his son.

WITH THE FLASHES OF THE
NIGHT / Phoebus Delphis

Again and again they discovered me
so I could sharpen my spirit
on the flint of lofty rocks
and so I could light my lamp
with the flashes of the night.

HE LIT HIS PIPE / Phoebus Delphis

He lit his pipe
not with the ashes of the past
but with the fire of reality.
His smoke was never of burned incense
but of the storm.

WINTER / Antal Vizy

The wind gripped the stiff mist tightly
and tore it with gnashing teeth.
Everything was clear then: the sky's blue seemed
like a bright glass knob
with a smiling face of streaked clouds.

Time walked among the plants with cautious steps
—as panthers go into the jungle—
and sparkling moments scattered on the snow
and the slow rhythm put everything to sleep.
The white earth closed its snow-eyes,
only the frost admired with staring eyes. . .

ON THE SITE OF THE
CONVENT / Tibor Tollas

A century ago the linden tree flourished,
The fountain played in the courtyard.
A white monk weeded the flowers
And the light husked the rosary of the rose.

A century ago, with humble kindness
Silent gestures illuminated manuscripts,
And the marks of times long past
Covered the yellow parchment pages.

Today pain groans, the cellar
Is a dark den where mold grows.
Manacles mourn for flesh. But now the mutilated hand

Covers the cell walls with inscriptions.
Under the broken apse these stones
Keep Europe together.

ON THE WATERSHED / Tibor Tollas

At sundown I reached the top of the ridge,
Two great oceans around us;
Our rivers seek their way
On the east and west slopes,
And I stand motionless on the wall of time.

I watch, as the last loyal soldier
Watched Pompeii crumble,
Both seas wash our shore;
So the Hungarian remains the only man
Neither Eastern nor Western.

FINALE / Tibor Tollas

Instead of leaf-covered branches, the morning bells
Tremble among the tree trunks in the garden.
And the dead leaves send a chill
Down our neck as they fall on our frostbitten hair.

Were they futile, the sorrows and desires of the years?
Under the bare trees' bark
The pulse of life forms rings
And at every moment ripens its fruit.

"Somebody died last night," the sick
Pale ones whisper, glancing timidly.
The flower of pure sadness
Lights up their faces over the short-lived years.

The cemetery poplars glow with a faint flash;
Not even night blots it out.
Indomitable life is born in pain,
Born because it had its death.

THE SHADE OF THE MAGNOLIA / Eugenio Montale

The shade of the Japanese magnolia
is scattered now that the purple buds
have fallen. A cicada whirrs
at intervals on the summit. It's no longer
the time of voices' harmony,
Clizia, the time of the deity
who devours his believers and reincarnates them.
It was easier to spend oneself, to die
at the first wingbeat, at the first encounter
with the enemy, a game. Now the harder way
begins: but not you, consumed
by the sun and rooted, and yet a downy
thrush flying high above the cold
wharves of your river—the shivering of frost
doesn't bend you, frail fugitive
to whom zenith nadir Cancer Capricorn
remained indistinct so that war
might be in you and in who adores in you
the prizes of your Husband. . . The others withdraw
and fall back. The lime which subtly
engraves will pass over in silence, the husk
of him who sang will soon be dust
of glass underfoot, the shade is livid—
it's autumn, it's winter, it's the sky
which leads you and in which I throw myself, a mullet
leaping in the dry wind under the new moon.

Good-by.

DAY AND NIGHT / Eugenio Montale

Even a flying feather can sketch
your figure, or the ray which plays hide-and-seek
among the furniture, the mirror's image
of a child, from the roofs. On the circle of walls
trails of smoke prolong the spires
of poplars and down on the rickety truck the knife grinder's parrot
ruffles its feathers. Then the sultry night
on the little square, and the footsteps, and always this hard
labor of sinking to rise just the same again
for centuries or moments, from nightmares which can't
recover the light of your eyes in the luminous
cave — and still the same cries and the long
weeping on the veranda
if suddenly a shot resounds which reddens
your throat and breaks you wings, O perilous
messenger of dawn
and the cloisters and hospitals awake
at a tearing of trumpets. . .

ON AN UNWRITTEN LETTER / Eugenio Montale

Is it for tingling sunrises, for a few
strands on which the tuft
of life is tangled and strung out
in hours and years that dolphins somersault
in pairs with their young today? Oh that I'd hear
nothing of you, that I could escape the flash
of your eyes. There are other things on earth.

I can't disappear or reappear; the vermilion
furnace of night is late
and evening lingers on;
prayer is torture and not yet
among the rising rocks has the bottle
reached you from the sea. The waves
break emptily on the cape at Finisterre.

SEASCAPE / Eugenio Montale

The wind rises, the dark is torn to shreds,
and the shadow you cast on the fragile
railing bristles. Too late

if you want to be yourself! The mouse
drops from the palm tree, the lightning's on the fuse,
on the long, long lashes of your gaze.

WHAT DO YOU WANT, SHEPHERD OF WIND? / Salvatore Quasimodo

And there's still the call of the old
shepherd's horn, harsh over the white
ditches of snakeskins. Perhaps
it gives breath to the plains of Acquaviva,
where the Platani rolls sea-shells
under the water between the feet of young
olive-skinned boys. O as for earth the gust
of imprisoned wind breaks and echoes
in the already crumbling light; what do you want,
shepherd of wind? Perhaps you summon the dead.
You do not hear with me, confused by the sea's
reverberation, attentive to the low cry
of fishermen lifting their nets.

STONE QUARRIES / Salvatore Quasimodo

Syllables of shadows and leaves,
on the grass in abandon
the dead make love.

I listen. Night is dear to the dead,
to me a mirror of sepulchres,
of stone quarries of deep green cedars,

of mines of rock-salt,
of rivers whose Greek name
is a verse to repeat, softly.

IN THE SENSE OF DEATH / Salvatore Quasimodo

Sky-blue trees
where the sweetest sound migrates
and taste is born in the fresh showers.

Gently the light
wavers in a branch
at its wedding with the wind;

in the sense of death,
here I am, frightened by love.

A BURIED ONE IN ME SINGS / Salvatore Quasimodo

I withdraw; the shade
of myrtles overwhelms
and hushed space lays me down.

Nor does love bring
glad harmonies of woods
in the lonely hour with me;
paradise and marsh
sleep in the heart of the dead.

And a buried one in me sings
who breaks the stone
like a root; and points to signs
of the opposite way.

WOODS ARE SLEEPING / Salvatore Quasimodo

Womb dried of love and birth,
I've mourned near you
for long years, uninhabited.

Woods are sleeping
with peaceful green, with wind,
plains where sulphur
was the summer of myths,
motionless.

You did not enter to give me life,
presage of lasting pain:
The earth died on the waters,
old hands in the rivers
gathered papyrus.

I cannot hate you: so light
my hurricane heart.

COOL WITH SLEEPING RIVERS / Salvatore Quasimodo

I find you in fortunate landing-places,
joined with the night,
now exhumed
like warmth of a new joy,
cruel grace of living without a river-mouth.

Virgin roads oscillate
cool with sleeping rivers:

And I'm still the prodigal who hears
his name out of the silence,
when the dead call.

And death
is a space in the heart.

SPACE / Salvatore Quasimodo

An equal radius encloses me
in a center of darkness,
and vainly I escape.
Sometimes a child (not mine)
sings there; the space is short
and smiles with dead angels.

It tires me. And love on earth
is good even if chasms boom there
with water, stars and light;
even if it awaits, a desert paradise,
its god of spirit and stone.

MIRROR / Salvatore Quasimodo

And here on the trunk
buds break:
a newer green than the grass
which rests the heart:
the trunk already seemed dead,
bent on the slope.

And everything tastes of wonder to me;
and I am that rain of clouds
reflecting today in the canals
its piece of bluer sky,
that green which splits the bark,
which wasn't even there last night.

IN THE WILLOW BRANCHES / Salvatore Quasimodo

And how could we sing
with the foreign foot on our heart,
among the dead abandoned in the piazzas
on the ice-hard grass, at the lamb-like
lament of the children, at the black moan
of the mother who went to meet her son
crucified on the telegraph pole?
In the willow branches, as a vow,
our lyres were also hung,
they swung lightly in the sad wind.

WE'VE HEARD THE SEA AGAIN / Salvatore Quasimodo

For several nights we've heard the sea again,
easy, back and forth along the smooth sands.
The echo of a voice which, shut in the mind,
comes back from time; and also this
unceasing lament of seagulls: perhaps
birds of the towers whom April
drives to the plain. Already
you were close to me with that voice;
and I wish there could also come to you
an echo of the memory of me now,
like that dark murmur of the sea.

THE CROSSING / Salvatore Quasimodo

Where do you call from? This mist resounds
faintly with you. From their kennels again,
it's time, the eager hounds rush forth
to the river on the scented trails:
shining with blood on the other bank
the polecat laughs derisively. I know
that crossing: there on the water
black stones rise; and how many boats
pass in the night with sulphur torches.
Now you're really far away
if your voice has the immeasurable tone
of an echo, and I scarcely hear its cadence.
But I see you: you hold violets
in your closed hands, so pale, and lichens
near your eyes. So you are dead.

VISIBLE, INVISIBLE / Salvatore Quasimodo

Visible, invisible
the driver on the horizon
in the arms of the highway calls,
answers the islands' voice.
I too don't go adrift,
the world rolls around, I read
my story as a night watchman
the rainy hours. The secret has fortunate
margins, stratagems, difficult attractions.
My life, cruel and smiling inhabitants
of my roads, of my landscapes,
is without door-knobs.
I'm not prepared for death,
I know the beginning of things,
the end is a surface where the invader
of my shadow travels.
I'm not acquainted with shadows.

THE INCOMPARABLE EARTH / Salvatore Quasimodo

For a long time I've owed you words of love:
or perhaps they are those which fall quickly
every day scarcely struck
and memory doubts them, which transforms
the inevitable signs into dialogue
the spirit's vertical enemy. Perhaps
the plunge of the mind doesn't make my words
of love heard or the fear
of the arbitrary echo which the feeblest
image of a tender sound
discloses: or they touch invisible
irony, its axelike nature
or my life already circumvented, love.
Or perhaps the color dazzles them
if they clash with the light
of time that will come to you when mine
will no longer be able to call obscure
love already lamenting
beauty, the impetuous break
with the incomparable earth, love.

NIGHT / Maria Celeste Achille Todde

The lighted candle moves
night spirits on the wall;
on the Armenian chest
three white calla lilies
shake their pistils
and their petals are like ghosts.

Deep in the shadow of the stems
your profile
emerges slightly.

Night's filled with the spirit's colors:
soon dawn will return your face
to me, marked with anxieties.
In daylight I'll lose
truths gathered from night's silence.

THE GREEN COMB / Raffaele Carrieri

No one says that May is here.
Not the sun that shows its rays
Nor the poplar with its rabbit-nose.
Your hand that rises and opens says so.
The open hand combing
With a green comb says so.
The falconer making his falcon swing,
The swan on the stream,
The maestro raising his baton
Surely draws no better music.

AS YOU WISH / Mario Luzi

The north wind cracks the clay,
it presses, it hardens the farmlands,
it disturbs the water in the basins; it leaves
hoes fixed, ploughs inert
in the field. If someone goes out for wood,
or changes places with difficulty or stops a while
shrunk up in cowl and cape,
he clenches his teeth. What prevails in the room
is the silence of the testimony
of the snow, the rain, the smoke,
of the immobility of change.

Here I put pine logs
on the fire, I listen
to the shuddering windows, I'm neither calm
nor anxious. You who come
through long promise and occupy the place
left by suffering
not to despair either of me or you,
search in the nearness of the house,
the grey door-frames.
Little by little the measure is filled,
little by little, little by little, as
you wish, the solitude overflows,
you come and enter, draw with downward hands.

It's a day of this year's winter,
one day, one day of our life.

THE HOLIDAY ENDED / Pier Paolo Pasolini

The holiday ended over a Rome
deaf to every simple expectation, night fell;
like trash caught on the wind, footsteps
return home, voices and whistles
die away far and wide through the streets
with their vacant alleys. It's supper time.
But where the city's chaos is congealed
in open fields and constellated lights
along the avenues walled within a peace
of death, the night's already old;
and sunk as in a tranquil
tomb, the city's chaos is congealed
on the mud the cyclist burns up lost
in his desolate race—a song
that echoes tenuously on the dirty wet
pavements . . . Then on the river road
dazzling crowns of headlights,
a star beside the clouds—
around the outskirts, from Monteverde
to Monte Testaccio, stagnating damp and exhausted,
a droning of workers' voices
and motors—a paper crust
of our world over the naked universe.

I REMEMBER A SEASON / Maria Luisa Spaziani

I remember a season up in the great
hills, worn by the breath
of the night north wind. A mulberry
moaned in tossing, so loud
its cry awakened me.

Yesterday when I returned to you it seemed
only a day gone by.
Inside the north wind raged.
Clinging to the balcony, intact, hung
an old crushed rose of mine.

FROM "THE WATERS OF SATURDAY" Maria Luisa Spaziani

Winter whistles around the steeple,
ten strokes toll in the dark.
The snow-plough rumbles: memory
has lost forever the ancient flutes,
the cabals of gestures, words
scattered in the wind.

All past events are mere dreams . . .

Even the ruined wall of your name
is softly covered by snow.

THE HIPPOPOTAMUS / Théophile Gautier

The broad-bellied hippopotamus
Inhabits Java's jungles where
More monsters than you've ever dreamed
Cry from the depths of every lair.

The boa, hissing, slinks away,
Close by, the tiger howls and creeps,
The angry buffalo stomps and sniffs—
In perfect calm he feeds and sleeps.

He watches man but keeps his ground,
He fears no blade or javelin
And laughs to feel the light rebound
Of hunters' bullets on his skin.

I'm like the hippopotamus:
With the conviction that I wear,
A hide nothing can penetrate,
I roam the wastes without a care.

CAT / **Charles Baudelaire**

Scholars and ardent lovers, when they grow old,
Admire the strong and gentle cat, for he
Like them enjoys the indoors and similarly
Is sedentary and sensitive to the cold.

A friend of learning with a sensual side,
The cat seeks silence and the darkness' spell.
He'd be the ideal funeral horse of hell
If such a task did not demean his pride.

Musing, he takes the noble attitude
Of some great desert Sphinx in solitude
Stretched out and slumbering in an endless dream.

His fertile loins have sparks of sorceries,
And bits of gold as fine as gold dust seem
Galaxies drifting in his mystic eyes.

DANCER / Edgar Degas

She dances as she dies, as around a reed,
To a flute where the sad air of Weber plays;
The ribbon of her footsteps writhes and twists,
Her body sinks and drops like a falling bird.

The violins drone. Cool, with the water's blue,
Sylvana comes and daintily flutters there.
The joy of coming alive and pure love play
Over her eyes, her breast, her whole new being.

And her satin feet embroider, like a needle,
Patterns of pleasure; and the springing girl
Tires my poor eyes straining to follow her.

But always with a nod the lovely mystery stops;
She draws her legs far backward as she leaps:
It's a frog leaping in Cythera's pools.

SPRINGTIME / Stéphane Mallarmé

The sickly spring has sadly driven away
Winter, bright winter, season of peaceful art,
And in my body where dull blood presides
Impotence stretches its limbs with a long yawn.

Colorless dawns grow warm under my skull
That's bound with an iron band like an old tomb,
And I wander sadly toward a vague, beautiful
Dream in the fields where boundless strength is flaunted.

Then I fall, weak from the smell of the trees, worn out,
And as I dig a grave in front of me in my dream,
Gnawing the hot soil where the lilacs grow,

I wait for my boredom to rise as I plunge down. . .
But the blue ridicules shrubs and resurrections,
With countless birds flourishing, twittering in the sun.

TWO FOOL'S SONGS / Émile Verhaeren

i

Break their paws and backs,
chase the rats, the rats;
and scatter the black wheat
at night
in the dark.

When my heart broke long ago
a woman picked it up
and gave it to the rats.

—Break their paws and backs.

I've seen them in the hearth,
ink spots on the wall,
nibbling on my death.

—Break their paws and backs.

I felt one of them
crawl on me one night
and gnaw at the bottom of the hole
where my heart was plucked
out of my chest.

—Break their paws and backs.

The wind blows through my head,
the wind that blows under the door,
and the black rats, up and down,
inhabit my dead skull.

—Break their paws and backs.

For we know nothing, nothing,
who cares about good and bad?
Ah, will you scatter black wheat
tonight
by handfuls in the dark?

ii

The black toad on the white ground
stares at me no doubt
with eyes bigger than his head;
he stole those eyes from me
when my face disappeared
one night when I turned my head.

My brother? He's a liar
with flour in his teeth;
he's over there with crossed arms and legs,
turning around,
turning in the wind
on that wooden mill.

The mill is my cousin
who used to be a vicar so dead-drunk on wine
the sun turned red with him;
I remember he lived in a shack
with dead men in his closets.

For our genitals
are a pair of pebbles
and our money's a sack of lice,
we three fools
who marry by the light of the moon
three madwomen on the dune.

LARKS / Saint-Pol-Roux

The clipping of scissors snips the air.

Now the crepe of mystery twilight ghosts drape over the cool flesh of life, now the crepe of the dark has stolen over the town and countryside.

The clipping of scissors snips the air.

Do you hear the good Lord's low bell cajole with the firebrand of its tolling the eyes, those yellow asphodels, the eyes crouched under the ashes of night?

The clipping of scissors snips the air.

Then rise from the dream in which we seem to be dead, my love, and adorn your window with the lilies, peaches and raspberries of your being.

The clipping of scissors snips the air.

Come up on the hill where the windmills charter their linen wings, come up on the hill where you can watch the divine diamond of the sky's enormous alliance spraying eternal sparks.

POEM / Pablo Picasso

Fire-tongue airs his face in the flute the cup that singing in him chafes the ever so lively stab of the blue that situated in the bull's gaze inscribed in his head adorned with jasmines waits for the sail to inflate the piece of crystal that the wind wrapped in the cape of the mandoble dripping with caresses distributes bread at random and to the lilac-colored dove and squeezes with all his spite against the flaming lemon's lips his crooked horn which frightens with its waves of good-bye the cathedral that crumbles in his arms without a hurrah while there blares in his face the radio roused by the dawn which photographing in its kiss a sun-bug consumes the perfume of the hour that falls and crosses the flying page undoes the bouquet that blows away furry between the sighing wing and the smiling fear the knife which skips with pleasure while leaving this very day floating as it likes and no matter how at the precise and necessary moment at the top of the well the cry of the rose which the hand flings to him like a pittance of alms.

FOREST / Jules Supervielle

Ten Indians surround me
Smoking my last cigars,
And I am diagonally
Penetrated by the long stares
Of their dark eyes piercing the dark
By strength of recognition.

Around the ring of Indians
I watch a little dog trot by—
Blind, with good-natured eyes
Of china-blue, wide open
As if for an offering
Since a cobra bit him.

Suddenly, sniffing and running
Against our feet and legs,
The dog smells out his former eyes
In the thick grass and under the plants,
Paws at the ground and goes up the trees
Like a performing dog.

And in the overripe night that falls
The ten Indians smoke in a circle,
The old chief loses a match
And, searching on the lawn for it,
Burns all the matches he has left
But doesn't find the one that's lost.

The blind dog turns around and around
To mark out a horizon for himself.

IGUAZU / Jules Supervielle

Across the pampas relieved only
by cattle condemned to graze from the first flicker of day
until the grass has a taste of sundown,
the threatening train rolls on, aiming all its iron at the
    Guarani north.
Suddenly there's a palm tree in the open plain,
an original palm, a palm in its own country,
the first sign of the approaching tropics,
then a little cluster of palms
facing on all sides,
then palms giving rise to others,
all forced by the furious train
to slip noiselessly into the background
in complete obedience,
everything that was ahead abruptly passing
from the forest, into memory,
and not obliged to live in me hereafter
except in the jumble of images the stubborn train shakes
like bills of fare, at inns, passed by uncertain hands.
But the forest gets so dense it has stopped the train.

Now on the river
the paddle-wheel boat and my thoughts float away
while ferry-boats slip past
covered with freshly cut cedars stiff as dead Indians;
we don't even hear the forest's breath
in the silent burned landscape.

The docked boat's steam-whistle cuts the countryside
cruelly with its notched knife.
The cataracts of the Iguazu,
under the stubborn presence of trees of all heights that want to
    see everything,
the cataracts
in a riot of white
charge in countless violent vertical
sprays as if they wanted
to penetrate the world.

The ropes where the spirit, a poor swimmer, clings
break at the level of the future.
Garbled phrases, dark surviving letters
search blindly for one another, drifting
to form islets of thought
and suddenly, as a commander takes a roll-call of his men after
    an alert,
I count my scattered selves whom I muster as quickly as possible.
Here I am again, complete,
watching my everyday hands.
And I close my eyes and cement my eyelids.

THE WORLD IN US / Jules Supervielle

Every object separated from its noise, its weight,
Always in its color, its reason and its race,
And precisely what it needs of light and space
That all may be agile and satisfied with its lot.
And all that lives and breathes and sings with me
—Inhuman objects as well as familiar ones—
And fed with my blood takes refuge in its warmth.
The mountain visits one day with the lamp,
Which shines, which is the greater in me?
Oh I know nothing more if I open my eyes,
My science lies in me behind my eyelids
And I know no more about it than my obscure blood.

LET'S SHIELD YOUR LIGHT WITH OUR HAND, MY HEART / Jules Supervielle

Let's shield your light with our hand, my heart
Pitilessly surrounded by the great lords of the Wind
Who delight in wanting to blow out this candle.
I go on, despite everything, amid their laughter
And always hope they will forget me a little.

I show my strength in the middle of my night.
This leaping horse is part of my eyes
He will return no more behind my eyelids
And, not suspecting who gave birth to him,
He looks around him, lost in his galloping,

But he lives on, look at him raising the dust.

MAKE ROOM / Jules Supervielle

Vanish a moment, make room for the landscape,
The garden will be beautiful as before the flood,
Without men, the cactus will be a vegetable again,
And you have nothing to see in the roots which seek
What will escape you, even with your eyes closed.
So let the grass thrust out beyond your dreams
And later you'll return to see what happened.

MEMORY / Jules Supervielle

When we shall hold our head between our hands
In a stony gesture, clumsily immortal,
Not like the saints—only like humble men—
When our love will be divided by our shadows,

If you ever dream of me I'll surely know it
In my head where only a gloomy wind will blow;
Above all, don't believe that I'm indifferent
If I should answer you by means of silence.

THE FACE / Jules Supervielle

In order to face the sky I need a face
Resembling only mine with its sparkling eyes
And to climb up the night I need this blue,
This memory of the day and my good mother
Crouched between my eyelashes with such reserve
That no one thinks of her, seeing their color.
She knows how to stand me with such patience
That she likes to mingle with my ignorance
And no one dreams that I am not alone
To leap at will in the bottomless well of the sky.
Forgive me for not having known, O kind resemblance,
How to imitate your reserve or keep your silence.

THE WORLD IS FULL OF VOICES. . . / Jules Supervielle

The world is full of voices of lost faces
That turn around day and night to ask for one.
I tell them, "Speak to me in familiar language,
For I'm uneasy in a large crowd."
"Don't compare our condition with yours,"
A voice answers, "I was called so-and-so,
I don't know my name any more, my brain is gone
And I can only prevail on that of others.
Let me depend a little on your thoughts.
It's a great deal like a living ear
For someone like me who scarcely exists.
Believe me, I'm nothing but a dead man,
I want to tell someone who weighs his words."

TIME'S HORSES / Jules Supervielle

Whenever the horses of Time stop at my door
I always hesitate and watch them drink
Since it's my blood with which they slake their thirst.
They face me with a gaze of recognition
While their long drafts fill me with feebleness
And leave me so fatigued, alone and deceived
That a brief passing night invades my eyelids
And suddenly makes me gather strength within me
So that some day when the thirsty team returns
I can still be alive and quench their thirst.

POSTHUMOUS / Jules Supervielle

We must give the dead everyday speech,
Words which pass easily from our lips to their ears,
Words to keep us company
When we're no longer alive.
Help me, men, my friends,
It's not a job for one alone,
With these common phrases polished by time,
Your speech and mine as well as our fathers'
Especially for the war dead
With their careers blown up,
Phrases chosen with care
To give them assurance.
Nothing is more afraid than a dead man
If he feels the outside air a little
That leaves him suspicious
Phrases we must hold ready
So they can move their lips
And finding them beautiful for having served so long
They feel the slight fever
Of one who once lost the memory of darkness
And looks ahead.

LIGHT, LIGHT, SOMEWHAT REVOLVING. . .
Jules Romains

Light, light, somewhat revolving, somewhat dulled!

The mist's and dampness' trial at motion which
Collects a heaven's matter from the pavements.

The day not yet arrived inspires the cloud.
Here all the world's best things are visible
That stir and torture and transform themselves.

All life's a prey to native apprehensions.
A kind of blue and rosy impetus
Entangles wisps of sleep with dragging rain.

But nothing moves in the bare branches. Scarcely
Does water tremble underneath the gate,
Or grasses ripple on the slopes, or farther,
Reflections strike a wall above the rampart.

What cession, what unravelling of all life!
Nothing prevents an avenue from unrolling
And falling from the city to the port.
The wagons, rumblings of the earth, the whispers
Of dreams escaped and running toward the ships!

The wind that walks this street is not asleep;
It's cold with sleeplessness, shakes with fatigue.
It takes you, though, and adds you to its anguish;
There is no clothing that will protect you;
There is no memory that's thick enough.
A gust, your heart's seized quickly like a heedless
Pedestrian who is left with empty cries.

> But O how sweet was restlessness,
> How full of joy was every sadness,

And how the bitterest morning wind
Had unction and benevolence!

How fine to tremble at the dawn!
How fine to live!

                                        and even perhaps

How good it will have been to die!

THE STAIN / Pierre Jean Jouve

I saw a thick green sheet of oil
Drained from an engine and for a long, long time
On the hot street in the squalid district
I dreamed of my mother's blood.

For white skin is a nocturnal expression
And what deserts have her diurnal feet not trod?
A shadow—what she is—is no more frightened
Nor more obscene, nor more terribly wicked.
The man without a sin
Is he who ought not to die, is therefore he
Who should know no inhibition, is therefore he
Who would have no equal, and therefore should not live.

THE STRAWBERRIES / Tristan Dérême

The strawberries on the white porcelain plate still yield
The chill, fresh smell of sunrise in the field,
Of boughs and moss and ice-encrusted streams.
I've laid upon the cloth your cluster of dreams,
And while you ponder with a thoughtful gaze
I watch among the leaves how the moon plays
As in old elegies on this somber night.
A pure warm breeze flickers the candlelight
Rocking the arbor where the vine-boughs weave
With the pale rose. Take strawberries. You perceive
Sugar dissolving in the golden wine;
Time on our brows spreads sugar powdered fine
And soon my hair will be thick, white and free.
What matter, if tonight you lean to me,
Fearless how red the leaf of autumn is,
And smother the lamplight reaching for my kiss.

Stay in your shell, then, snail-like and oppose
This moist perfume of apricot and rose;
Your solitude adorned with dreams may yet
Be sweet; it rains; your horns are getting wet.
The sod is crushed under the hot rain's lash,
The house is brightened by the thunder flash
Which lights the wall where you cling close behind
Cobwebs; the stars were blown out by the wind;
The moon, like fruit, has tumbled over the lawn.
Pull in your horns; with noise and lightning gone,
In self reflection gild your reveries.
Outside the storm crumples the grass and trees,
Rattles the slates and makes the roof resound.
Let the world fall to ruin all around!

ON A PICTURE BY A CHINESE PAINTER
Henri Michaux

A flock of birds swoops over the valley
With a gust from the sky
with a thick lenticular tumult
the squadron rises
There's a vast whiteness
above
below
sideways
everywhere
a mourning white
Busy trees search for their boughs torn off and
splintering distracted trees
trees like bloody nervous systems
but no human beings in this drama
The humble man doesn't say "I'm unlucky"
the humble man doesn't say "We suffer
our loved ones die
our people are homeless"
He says "Our trees suffer"

AT THE FLORIST'S / Jacques Prévert

A man enters a florist's
and picks out some flowers
the girl wraps up the flowers
the man puts his hand in his pocket
to get the money
money to pay for the flowers
but at the same time
suddenly
he clutches his heart
and he falls

At the same time that he falls
the money rolls on the ground
and then the flowers fall
at the same time as the man
at the same time as the money
and the girl stands there
with the rolling money
with the broken flowers
with the dying man
obviously that's all very sad
and she ought to do something
that florist
but she doesn't know how to set about it
she doesn't know
where to begin

There are so many things to do
with that dying man
those broken flowers
and that money
that money that rolls and rolls
and never stops rolling.

ON A NIGHT WITHOUT ADORNMENT / René Char

Look at the night beaten to death; continue to let it suffice for us.

At night the poet, drama and nature become only one, but on the rise and aspiring.

Night bears nourishment, the sun refines the nourished part.

At night our apprenticeships remain in a state of serving still others after us. Fertile is the freshness of this guardian!

Infinity attacks but a cloud saves.

Night affiliates itself with any instance of life inclined to end in spring, to fly away in a storm.

Night takes on a rust color when it consents to hold the iron gates of its gardens ajar to us.

To the gaze of the living night, dream is sometimes only a spectral lichen.

It wasn't necessary to inflame the heart of night. It was necessary that darkness be master where the morning dew is chiseled.

Night follows only itself. The solar belfry is only an interested toleration of night.

Night it is that sees to the renewal of our mystery; night it is that performs the robing of the chosen.

Night sharpens our human past, bows its psyche before the present, puts indecision in our future.

I shall be filled with a celestial earth.

Plenary night where ungracious dream blinks no more,
keep what I love alive for me.

THE INVENTORS / René Char

They came, the rangers of the other side, those unknown to us,
    the rebels to our customs.
They came in great numbers.
Their band appeared at the dividing line of the cedars
And from the field of ancient harvests hereafter watered and
    green.
The long march had overheated them.
Their caps broke over their eyes and their foundered feet were
    stuck in the waves.
They noticed us and stopped.
Obviously they didn't expect to find us there,
On fertile lands and well-enclosed fields,
Wholly indifferent to an audience.
We raised our brows and encouraged them.

The most eloquent one drew near, then a second one just as
    uprooted and cumbersome.
We came, they said, to warn you of the impending arrival of
    the hurricane, your implacable foe.
We don't know him any more than you do
Except by reports and ancestral secrets.
But why are we unaccountably happy before you and suddenly
    like children?

We thanked and dismissed them.
But earlier they drank and their hands trembled and their eyes
    laughed around the edges.
Men of trees and axes, able to resist some terror but unfit to
    direct water, lay out buildings or cover them with pleasant
    colors,
They would ignore the winter garden and the economy of joy.

Surely we could have persuaded them and conquered them,
For the hurricane's distress is moving.
Yes, the hurricane was going to come soon;
But was that worth the trouble they spoke of and which turned
    the future upside down?
There is no urgent fear here where we live.

PUT ON GUARD / René Char

On our temperate side we have a series of songs in us, guarding us, wings of communication between our calm breath and our highest fevers. Rather trite pieces, mild in style and backward in form, yet wearing a small scar on their surface. Everyone has a right to establish a beginning and an end to this contestable glow.

At a time when death, docile to treacherous enchanters, defiles the loftiest chances, we don't hesitate to set free every moment at our command. Or better still, let us turn toward the morning-glory, that bindweed which night's final hour refines and opens but which noon condemns to be closed. It would be unusual if the quietude, on the other side of which it welcomes us precariously, were not what we had desired for a siesta.

ANOUKIS AND LATER JEANNE / René Char

I shall discover you in those I love, like a long flash of sheet lightning, as unaccountably as you appeared to me, Jeanne, when one morning confining yourself to your drawing, you led us from one rock to another to that end of ourselves we call a summit. Your face half hidden by your folded arm, your fingers entreating your shoulder, at the end of our climb you offered us a city, sufferings and the title of a genius, the disordered surface of a desert, and the wary bend of a river on whose shore builders questioned one another. But I returned to you quickly, Faucille, for you consumed your offering. And neither time nor beauty nor chance which unbridles our hearts could be measured with you.

Then I revived my ancient wealth, all our wealth, and commanding today what I will destroy tomorrow, I remembered that you were Anoukis the Hugger as fantastically as you were Jeanne, my best friend's sister, and as unaccountably as you were the Stranger in the spirit of that poor bell-ringer whose father used to say over and over that van Gogh was mad.

SENTRY OF THE SILENT / René Char

The stones crowded together in the wall and men
lived on the stones' moss. The heart of night
carried a rifle and women no longer lay in childbirth.
Dishonor had the look of a glass of water.

I've joined in the courage of a few pèople, I've
lived violently, without aging, with my mystery in
their midst, and I've trembled at the existence of
all other beings, like a leaky boat floating over
partitioned depths.

A WOMAN BROUGHT NAKED FACE TO FACE WITH THE SKY / Pierre Emmanuel

A woman brought naked face to face with the sky
and half-opened by the pale blue steel of silence
displays her blood on the stairway of my years
(Death alone agrees with those hard steps
built deliberately so that She would be killed on them)

This blood is beautiful with the plain white walls
beautiful with the sun that's reflected there unconcerned
beautiful with the nakedness of women who tread on it:
it foams and fondles their light feet
like lace at the foot of a summer evening.

THE ART OF POETRY / Pierre Emmanuel

Thousands of years of fine sand
That's the age of the new dawn
A thousand parchment dunes
From the wrinkles of my brow

This man who tramps about
In the cold of the first morning
Sees the dove go far away
And the garden vanish

Lost paradise of images
Every day my hand rewrites you
But tears up page after page
Your ink-stained dream

And beyond the wall my speech
Dust or pollen flies out of reach

PLEDGES / Pierre Emmanuel

This blood will never dry up on the earth
And these slaughtered dead will stay unburied.
We'll grind our teeth by strength of being silent.
We'll not weep over those inverted crosses.

But we shall remember these dead without memory.
We shall count our dead as they have been counted.
Those who weigh so heavy in the balance of history
Are astonished tomorrow that they are considered light.

And those who were killed for fear of being understood,
Their silence will not be forgiven any more.
Those who stood up to argue and pretend
Will be condemned even by the least pious men.

These dead, these simple dead, are our whole heritage;
Their poor bloody corpses will remain undivided.
We shall not let their image lie fallow—
Orchards will flourish on the greening meadows.

Let them be naked under the sky like our earth,
And let their blood be mixed with the well-loved springs.
The eglantine will cover with angry roses
The fierce spring seasons roused by this blood.

Let these spring seasons be unspeakably gentle to them:
Full of birds, songs, and children on roads.
And like a forest sighing around them
May a great multitude pray softly, lifting their hands.

LONDON, MARCH 1945 / Pierre Emmanuel

In the cemetery of Royal Hospital Road
The grass seems almost as old as the graves.
Around us with flaxen beards and red tunics stroll
(Old toys we put aside when evening falls)
The veterans of some forgotten wars.
A helmet yawns over a grave. The face
Of the dead soldier is a cave in which the past
Grows narrower like the echo of a shell:
Only the antenna of ants is still stirred by it.

Faces of the living which penetrate the stone
Sealed, compact, rough slabs laid over wells
Whose jealous water is wary of the light:
Prostitutes more patient than death
Long rows watching for something indescribably sad
A bus, the Queen Mother or even death;
Husky-voiced tub thumpers spouting laughs
At Marble Arch where girls go off in pairs
To sing a psalm and abandon themselves on the lawns
To some misadventurous lover, even more disgraceful
Than they, and taking vengeance with those gentle
Strangling hands, suddenly enormous

                                        (The spider
Is lost in the grass, and the slim hands are appeased
Until some beautiful evening the illuminating spasm
Of the other flesh reappears to haunt them: and press
Their thumbs tenderly on the too naked image
Whose throat is whiter than moonlight through the trees)

The double-deck buses lurch in the narrow streets
Brushing past the apartments. O gaze
To the point of disgust at a series of so many intimacies
Whose bricks are porous to fear, then at the decayed
City exposing its gums that are bruised
And blood-stained by the dust of those bricks.

Millions go away in pairs without reason
And others go alone without reason: the former want
To throw their leaden counterweight overboard
The others want to founder in a bare breast. The spring-water
Of the first lies stagnant in the others' hearts. Only tears
Clusters of black grapes refresh the city
But tears and rain winds and rumbling
Have a salt still stirring the unquenchable thirst
That suckles only lightning from the clouds. I drink
The crowd whose concern is drained by the streets,
Only your deserts are left to slake my thirst
O footprints, shifting sands where the alien moves
A sleepwalker in a dream using up his day.

Who knows how to set him on his course again? None.
Will one lost man go to another and ask
For that road which is forgotten, groping
And winding without ever reaching around the heart?
London, O skein entangled in the fog
Everyone hurries the thread of his life, and happiness
Snaps

      You would be lost, Lord, in these alleys
Where beyond the walls emaciated by winter
Yet wretched and haggard as a blind man's eyes
Someone (maybe I) waits and despairs
Of hearing his last, his only chance approaching in the distance!
The morning light brought in by your bright footsteps.

A GOOD-BY / **Alain Bosquet**

I won't see you any more
there's a sea to empty
there's a sky to dress
your face already reaches the trees
and for fifteen centuries
I'll look for your laugh
under objects of prey
I won't see you any more
there's a moon to gather
there's this space and others
to lodge in my veins
your knees roll under the river
your collarbones shine
on the rind of cliffs
I won't see you any more
there's a death to deceive
there's the planet to bite
with the countless teeth absence has given me

A NAIL FOR HANGING THE SOUL / Alain Bosquet

A doubt for rusting the body.
He throws himself like a die:
he rolls under the table.
Could he be only an overcoat
for his skeleton that follows after him?
For how many years has this old hat
replaced his skull?
Non-being is the abuse of being.
He gives the ludicrous one last chance.

HE INVENTS A VERTIGO / Alain Bosquet

He marches in himself to scatter himself better.
A colt loves him too much,
a mare thinks nothing of him.
How many patinas are needed for the soul?
Suns follow in their course
like scarabs on his shoulder.
An absence has changed its shell.
He fondles a stone,
finding a few doves there by mistake.

THE SUN IS A GLOBE OF FIRE / Antonio Machado

The sun is a globe of fire,
the moon is a mulberry disk.
A white dove alights
on the tall century-old cypress.

The parterres of myrtles seem
like faded powdery wool.
Flower garden and quiet evening.
The spray plays in the marble fountain.

TELL ME IF YOU REMEMBER, LOVE
Antonio Machado

Tell me if you remember, love,
those tender, lazy
yellow reeds
that lay in the dry ditch.

Do you remember the poppy
that summer pulverized,
the withered poppy,
black crepe over the prairie?

Do you remember the morning sun,
low and motionless,
shining and trembling, broken
on a frozen fountain?

THE AFTERNOON WILL YET. . . / Antonio Machado

The afternoon will yet
offer gold incense to your prayer,
and maybe the noon of a new day
will diminish your lonely shadow.

But your festival isn't the far away blue of the sea,
only the hermitage by the gentle river;
your sandals will not walk the drowsy
plain, nor the monotonous sand.

The green, holy, flowering earth
of your dreams is very close,
rosemary; very close, pilgrim
who scorn the shaded path
and the water of the wayside inn.

TAVERN GUITAR PLAYING A JOTA TODAY. . . / Antonio Machado

Tavern guitar playing a jota today,
a petenera tomorrow,
according to whoever comes and strums
your dusty strings,

guitar of the roadside inn,
you never were nor will you be a poet.

You're a soul uttering its lonely
harmony to passing souls. . .

And whenever a traveler hears you
he dreams of hearing a tune of his native town.

OH, FIGURES ON THE PORTICO. . .
Antonio Machado

Oh, figures on the portico, more humble
and distant every day:
ragged beggars
on marble stairways;

wretched sovereigns
of holy eternities,
hands rising from old cloaks
and tattered coats.

Did some illusion pass your way,
appearing
in the more peaceful hours
of the cold shining dawn?

On your black coat your hand
was a white rose.

INSECTS / Dámaso Alonso

To José Maria de Cossío

I get terribly annoyed by insects, I
absolutely distrust insects, I
get suspicious of all those signals, those heads and feet
    and those eyes,
especially those eyes
that keep me from warding off my fear at night,
in the awful dryness of night when insects
buzz around, on nights of insects
when I suddenly doubt they're around and I ask myself,
    are there really insects?
when insects buzz around and around and around,
when my soul completely aches with insects,
with all those feet and eyes, with all those little worlds
    of my life
where I've been suffering in the insects
when they buzz around and fly and dive in the water, when. . .
oh whenever insects.

At night the insects come out of the earth and out of my
    insect flesh
and gnaw on ashes and nibble away on me.
Dried insects, dried and mounted insects!
Item: dried insects that used to buzz around and nibble
    and dive in the water.
oh, on creation, on creation day,
when they nibbled on the leaves of the insects, of the
    trees of the insects
and nobody anywhere saw the insects that nibbled and nibbled
    away on the world,
the world of my flesh (and the flesh of insects),
the insects of the world of nibbling insects.

They came in many colors, those insects: green, yellow,
    the color of the date, the color of dry clay,
hidden, buried—outside the insects and inside my
    flesh, inside the insects and outside

my soul—
disguised as insects.
And with laughing eyes and laughing faces and feet
(the feet didn't laugh) the metallic insects nibbled and
nibbled and nibbled and nibbled on my poor soul,
buzzing and nibbling the corpse of my soul that didn't
    nibble and buzz,
nibbling and buzzing around my poor soul that didn't buzz,
    no, but finally nibbled, feebly nibbled,
nibbling and nibbling this metal world and these metallic
    insects that nibble my world of little insects,
that nibble my world and my soul,
that nibble my soul made of little metallic insects,
that keep nibbling my world and my soul, my soul. . .
oh the insects,
those damned insects!

POSITION / **Blas de Otero**

I like Walt Whitman for his doughty beard
and for his fine expansive poetry.
I am in full agreement with his voice,
and in accord with his great open heart.

I listen to Nietzsche. Night after night I read
a lively part of Sils-Maria. It sounds
with the gloomy sea. But what a good seasickness,
what a splendid gloom, how full!

I shun the man who has sold his honesty
and dreams by a sun which joins man
with death. Godless, he can't
help a sky rise above such rubbish.

Poor mortal creatures. Sad immortal creatures.
Spain, my homeland tangled up in tears.
Rivers of tears. Caudal weeping.
This is the place where I suffer. And sing.

THREE POEMS ON DEATH / Carlos Bousoño

1

There are times when we men write
sad poems dedicated to death.
It lurks there in our skeleton,
hard, firm, waiting.

And yet men never know it.
Death floats between their lips,
and as they watch the changing skies
they talk of love and everlasting songs.

But the bone at the bottom of their lives
restlessly waits for earth and death.
It's peaceful because light doesn't inhabit
its timeless place of rest.

I know the same things bones know,
and yet I stare
at the clean wind and sigh in it
without sadness, and sometimes I love.

2

Only the bones are eternal.
They are death waiting for its kingdom,
death that realizes it is sovereign
there in its lonely pit.

Bones are ancient. We human beings
know nothing of their origin,
but sunk in our body there lives in us
what we'll be underground.

Not the seed of the winds
nor the joy of things covered with light,
but a hard inscrutable skeleton
unredeemed and silent under the stars.

3

Maybe our bones were rock,
a mountain, a river, a fire or a valley
before man had appeared
like a pain under the winds.

For that reason the bone is a desire
to be a clean bodiless space once more,
and deep inside a hard autumn seems to go on,
a sad inexplicable autumn.

But the bones send their heavy wave
up to the eyes which are unaware,
and believing in the happiness of its white foam
we meet death under the endless sky.

THE DIFFICULT POEM / José Agustín Goytisolo

The poem is inside
and doesn't want to get out.

It pounds in my head
and doesn't want to get out.

I shout, I tremble,
and it doesn't want to get out.

I call it by name
and it doesn't want to get out.

Later down in the street
it stands before me.

THE TRANSLATION SERIES

brings to English-speaking readers the best of traditional and modern writing from around the world. This edition was prepared under the editorial supervision of BkMk Press, the College of Arts and Sciences, University of Missouri-Kansas City.

Other Books From BkMk Press

Artificial Horizon, by Laurence Gonzales. Short stories. $8.95.

Missouri Short Fiction, edited by Conger Beasley, Jr. 23 stories by Missouri writers. $7.95.

In the Middle, edited by Sylvia Griffith Wheeler. Poems and essays by ten Midwestern women poets. $9.50.

Modern Interiors: lithographs & confessions, by Stephen Gosnell. $12.95.

Writing in Winter, poetry by Constance Scheerer. $5.25

Selected Poems of John Knoepfle. $6.50.

The Selected Poems of Mbembe Milton Smith. $8.95.

Dark Fire, by Bruce Cutler. A book length narrative poem. $6.25.

Tanks, by John Mort, winner of Missouri Short Fiction Contest, 1985. Short fiction set in Vietnam. $8.95.

From BkMk's Translation Series

Wild Bouquet, by Harry Martinson (Swedish Nobel Laureate). Poetry and original drawings by the poet. Introduction by William Jay Smith. Translated by William Jay Smith and Leif Sjöberg, $10.95, casebound.

Hi-Fi and The False Bottom, by Goran Stefanovski. Two plays by a well-known Yugoslavian playwright, translated from the original Macedonian, with an introduction by James McKinley. $8.50.

Just When You Think You've Seen It All . . .

. . . *there's something new*

New Letters double issue, with fiction by Daniel Stern, a memoir by Lisel Mueller and "The Crossbow Cycle" by Pulitzer-Prize winner Peter Viereck; memorial sections to John Ciardi and Tom McAfee and much more . . .

New Letters special fiction issue: Delightful Stories of Deception and Decay, by Joyce Carol Oates, Harry Mark Petrakis, Speer Morgan and others (Summer 1986) . . .

New Letters Awards Issue, featuring prize-winning fiction, poetry and essays from the 1986 New Letters Literary Awards national competition, (Fall 1986) . . .

And remember, tune in **New Letters on the Air,** the best writers on radio, weekly on your local National Public Radio station (half-hour cassettes available at \$7.50 each. Catalogue free).

Lucy Masterman